To Ryder & Wyatt,
Bethanie & Benen
Happy reading.
Nancy Kelly Allen
2023

# BUGS ON THE JOB

By Nancy Kelly Allen

Illustrator Martyna Nejman

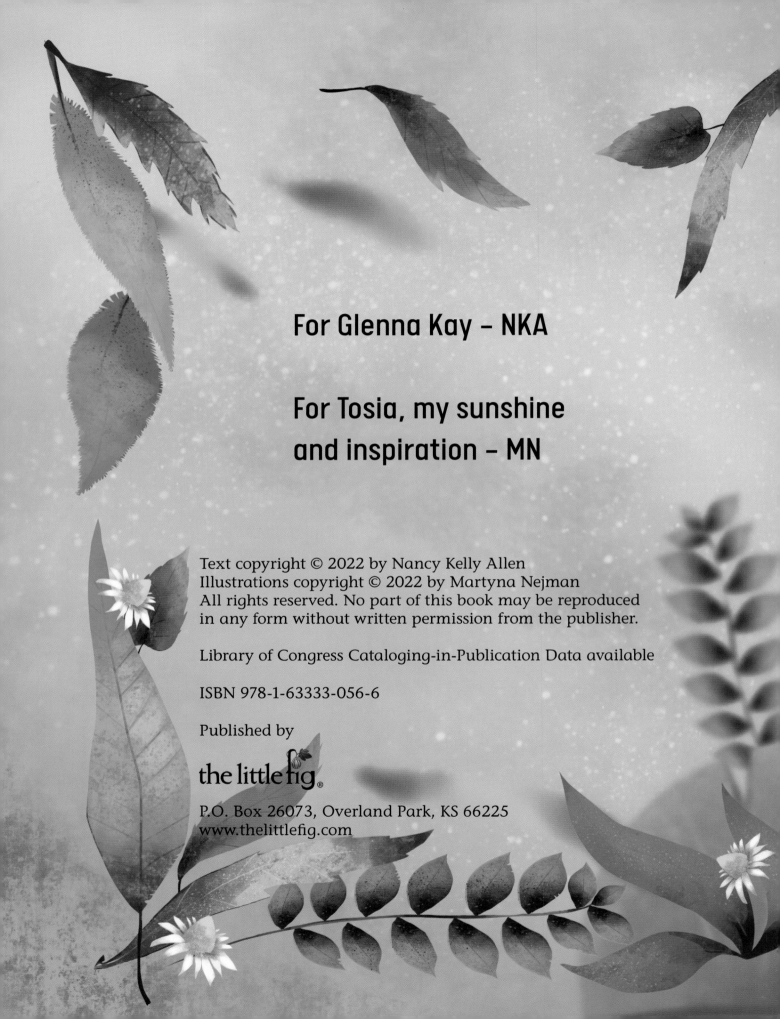

For Glenna Kay – NKA

For Tosia, my sunshine
and inspiration – MN

Library of Congress Cataloging-in-Publication Data available

ISBN 978-1-63333-056-6

Published by

the little fig.

P.O. Box 26073, Overland Park, KS 66225
www.thelittlefig.com

First up are the **decomposers**, nature's own forest rangers. These stag beetles work the night shift.

**Ian Sect:** "TREE"-mendous work.

**Ian Sect:** Out in the field we have dung beetles. What's the poop?
**Dung Beetle:** We munch and crunch on dung, better known as animal droppings, scat, or poo.
**Ian Sect:** What?!
**Dung Beetle:** Yep! Our job is to save the land from being piled up with you-know-what.
**Ian Sect:** Super scoopers!

**Ian Sect:** Now with the latest news on **pollinators**, those bugs that pick up pollen dust from a plant here and spread it to another, there.

**Ian Sect:** Bingo! Pollination. Flowers bloom.

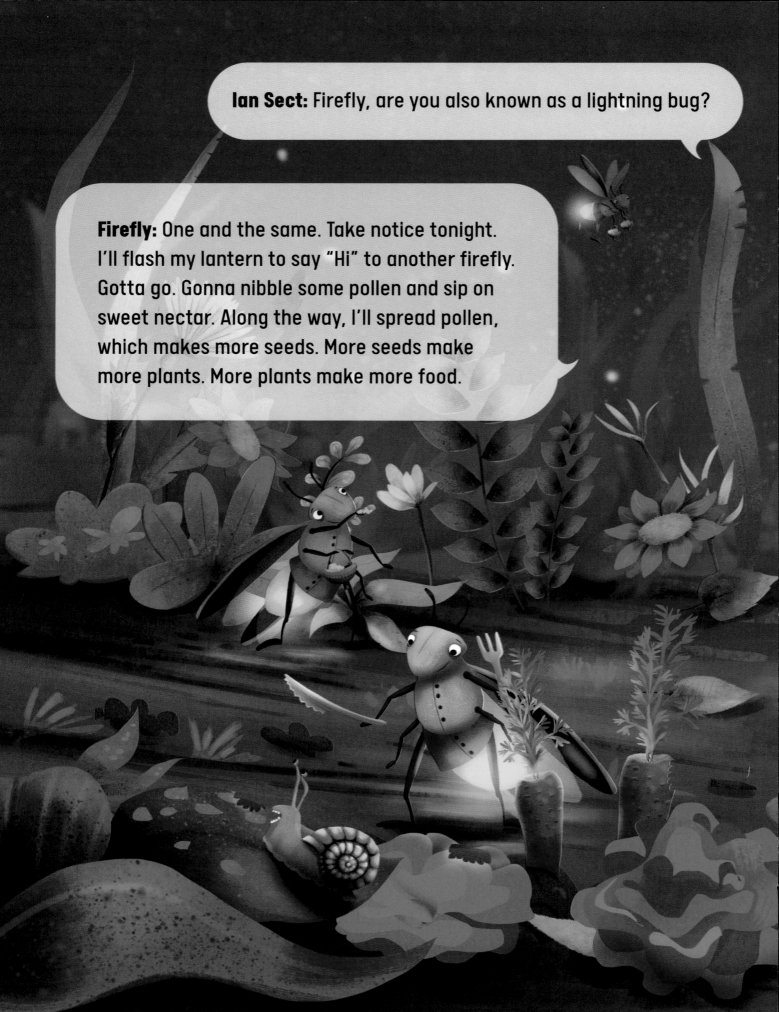

Ian Sect: De-"LIGHT"-ful!

Hey, reader! Firefly larvae live in moist areas. They gobble snails and slugs that chomp on garden plants like me.

**Ian Sect:** A hoverfly lives up to its name. It hovers in place like a helicopter.

**Hoverfly:** Flowers with bright colors are like a welcome mat to me. Watch me dart and dive for sweet food called nectar. Pollen sticks to my body. I hover, then dart to another flower. Yeah, a little pollen spills.

**Ian Sect:** Don't swat! They're the good guys.

My clusters of blazing color tell hoverflies, "Dinner's ready! The nectar is here." Ya-ya, baby, I welcome these bugs.

**Ian Sect:** I'm watching ladybugs eat. They say that's their job.

**Ladybug:** Yes, little ladybugs have big appetites. We scatter pollen as we fly and crawl. The bright colors and scents of flowers help us find pollen and nectar. And aphids! Aphids are itsy bitsy, green insects that chew on plants people need for food.
I chomp 20, 40, 50 aphids a day! BURP! Excuse me.

**Ian Sect:** Long live ladybugs.

Sometimes aphids try to eat me. Pesky pests! Ladybugs are my heroes.

**Ian Sect:** Butterflies flit and flutter like wind dancers. What a fun job!

**Butterfly:** Did you know some red and yellow flowers show secret patterns under special light? We call them nectar guides. As we sip nectar, pollen sticks to our bodies. Flying to other plants shakes the pollen off. Ta-da! **Pollination.**

**Ian Sect:** Butterfly, flutter by.

I'm one of those flowers that uses a pattern of ultraviolet light to show nectar to butterflies. I'm talking secret code here. SHHHHHH!

**Ian Sect:** Honeybees also collect nectar and turn it into something yummy. Honey! "BEE"-utiful!

**BEE:** Thousands of us bees live in a hive with our mother, the queen. Some bees build. Some care for the young. Others find food. We waggle dance—wiggle, wiggle, waggle—to tell other bees where to find flowers. Working together, we make enough honey to survive over winter and feed our young.

**Ian Sect:** That's the buzz on bees.

My flat petals make it easy for bees to land on me. Hello, Honey!

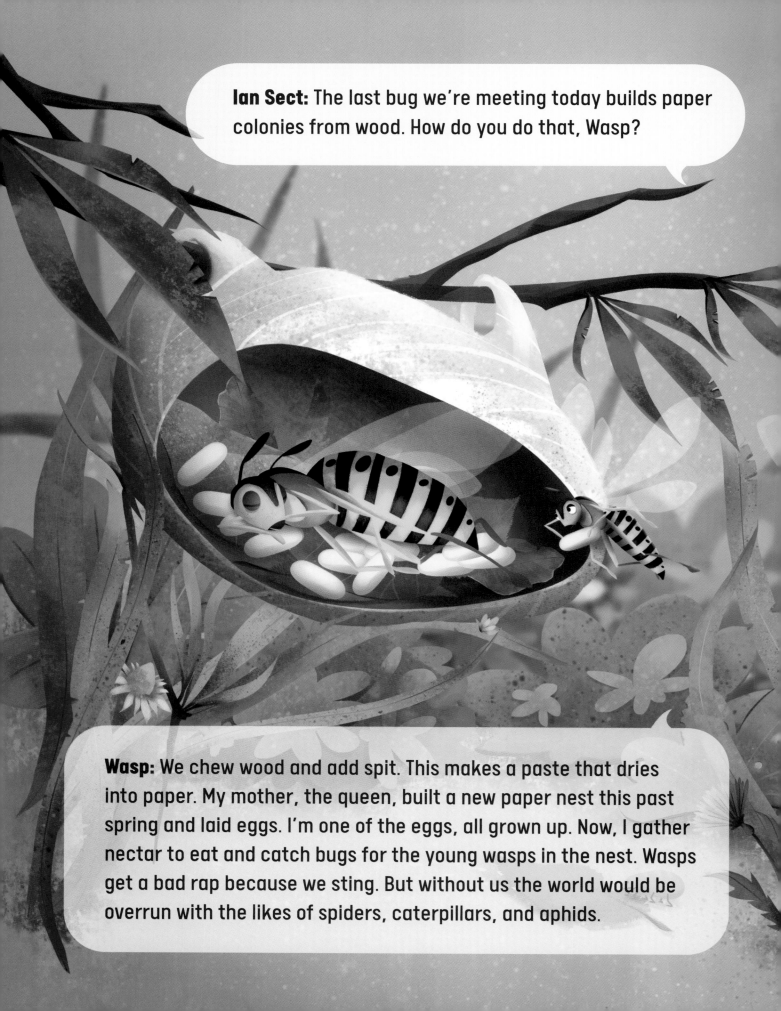

**Ian Sect:** The last bug we're meeting today builds paper colonies from wood. How do you do that, Wasp?

**Wasp:** We chew wood and add spit. This makes a paste that dries into paper. My mother, the queen, built a new paper nest this past spring and laid eggs. I'm one of the eggs, all grown up. Now, I gather nectar to eat and catch bugs for the young wasps in the nest. Wasps get a bad rap because we sting. But without us the world would be overrun with the likes of spiders, caterpillars, and aphids.

That's all from Ian Sect, reporting for RBUG in Bug Land with bugs on the job.

**Cute as a bug.** Bugs are insects. They have three parts: head, thorax, and abdomen. Over one million different types of insects share our world. Nearly half are beetles.

**Don't bug the bugs.** Most bugs are not harmful to people. Leave them alone so they can spread pollen. Pollinated plants make seeds that grow into more plants. We need plants. They produce much of the foods we eat.

**What's for lunch?** Bugs recycle dead trees and wood by eating them. The nutrients (matter that makes soil healthier) are returned to the ground. So, plants grow bigger and stronger.

**Sniff out the facts.** Bugs also recycle dead animals and animal droppings by eating them. If they didn't, dead animals and dung would pile up.

**Grab a bite to eat.** Everything needs food. Bugs eat nectar and pollen made by plants. Bugs also eat other bugs. And bugs are food for other animals.

Hey, Reader, let's show some love to the bugs! Without bugs we plants couldn't survive, and without plants, neither could you.

# Fun Facts about Bugs

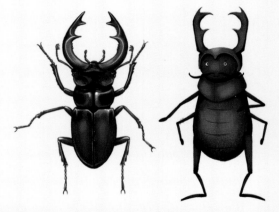

**Stag beetles** are named for their mandibles (jaws) that look like antlers on a stag (male deer). In olden days, people thought stag beetles could summon thunder and lightning. That's electrifying!

**Dung beetles.** Dung is both food and drink for these beetles. They roll the poo into balls, bury it, then either eat it themselves or lay their eggs in it. Larvae that hatch in the poo ball eat their way out as they grow.

**Fireflies** flash their yellow, orange, or green lights on warm, summer evenings. The body part that produces the light is called the lantern. Sometimes, thousands of fireflies light up at the same time in the same pattern. All together now: **Blink on**. Blink off. **Blink on.** Blink off. Nature's own light show.

**Carrion beetles** are also known as burying beetles. Their flat bodies allow them to crawl under dead animals and dig the soil out from underneath, burying their dead dinner for later.

**Hoverflies** have a yellow and black pattern, which makes them look like bees even though they are flies. How do you tell the difference? Hoverflies have one pair of wings; bees have two. Hoverflies get their name because they can hover in midair. They can even fly backwards.